Poems
I Wrote
When I
Wasn't
Talking

Janice O'Brien

Poems I Wrote When I Wasn't Talking
Copyright © 2015 by Janice O'Brien

ISBN: 978-0-9964672-7-8

Gemini Moon Press
First Edition, August, 2015
Printed in the United States of America

Cover/Interior design: Janice O'Brien
Poems in this book were set in Palatino 10/12.

A collection of poems about life, love, family, death and
some things in between.

janiceobrien.com

Ink runs from the corners of my mouth.
There is no happiness like mine.
I have been eating poetry.
                              ~ Mark Strand

Table of Contents

Expressing Gratitude

Thank you Janice Newman! If Janice hadn't given me an article about things to do when we lost power, (*Snowstorm October, 2011 Connecticut*) I may never have gone back to writing poetry.

Gratitude to my dear friend and mentor, Sindiwe Magona, giving me the best advice, "just write!" Appreciation to my long time writing pals, Irene Kriscinusis, Lori Amada Samuels, Hope Supris and Kitty Torres. Thank you to my new writing friend, Gerri O'Gorman Lambert, who pushed me to get my poems into print.

Thanks to my talented teachers at Main Line School Night, Amelia Bentley, Timothy Leonido and Barbara Corbo who, each in their own way, introduced me to Contemporary Poetry.

A special shout out to Imran Posner and Jools, my encouragers and supporters. And most importantly, thank you to my amazing daughters, Joy and Robin, who inspire me daily.

Love

The Mango

A crimson mango
sat still in a glass bowl
on my window sill
I'm not certain if it's ready to eat
I have no skill
judging luscious fruit
knowing if it's ripe or not
I ate a mango long ago
when a kind man I once loved
sweetly served it to me
one Sunday afternoon
He cut the mango with elegant precision
trimming its thick, gold flesh away
from the flat pit and burgundy skin
Juice ran down his thick brown hands
as he told stories about his favorite mango tree
in Jamaica when he was a school boy
My first bite, a delicious surprise
richer than a peach
sweet, exotic like papaya
Anticipating the taste from that day
I pick the mango from its bowl
slicing it as best as I can
my eyes closing
daydreaming of that island place.

Honorable Mention, The Newtowner, Winter 2013

Bridge of Love

Romantic souls
passionate lovers
seeking protection
of fervent love
march to the bridge
not any bridge,
Pont des Arts
Bridge of Love
search for a guarantee
symbolic promise of
unending and undying adoration

Sweethearts armed with
metal padlocks
inscribed love locks
fastened to the bridge
fling keys into a dirty Seine
romantic devotees
defending their definition of forever.

Note: June 2, 2015, Paris: The padlocks on the sides of the Pont des Arts were removed by city workers today because the weight of the over 700,000 locks caused damage to the bridge. At this time there is no plan to retrieve the keys from the River Seine.

Bring Me the Sunset

Bring me the sunset in a cup…
remember to collect fireflies in your pail
as a sapphire night becomes our blanket
under a sea of stars, entertained by the Milky Way
tenderness spills from our lips on mountain tops

Bring me the sunset in a cup…
gather daisies along the path
tie them with a green silk bow
remind me of the moment we fell in love
obsessed with everlasting and forever

Bring me the sunset in a cup…
carry the glass jar filled with strawberry jam
to savor as we did at Café Saint-Germain
when students created *bavardages bruyants*[1]
only my heart heard your words of endearment

Bring me the sunset in a cup…
deliver me a crescent moon in a velvet pouch
lighten my day, secure my night, strengthen my spirit
arm me to face regret alone
while shattered promises fall from weeping clouds

[1] *loud chatter*

Family

Wedding China

Feeling sad washing Mom's fine china
in warm, sudsy water
cherished, delicate
wedding plates, bowls
dainty pink and blue flowers
encircled with 14- carat gold

Prisoners locked in the cabinet
receiving parole
Thanksgiving, Christmas, Easter
not even my birthday
that June day paper plates carried
cake to the front lawn

Given to the groom and bride
an intimate ceremony during war
a small affair while friends and family
were overseas risking lives
wounded or worse
fighting for their country

Revered china sheltered
salad plates gifted from Aunt Babs
soup bowls from Georgia cousins
settings from in-laws
service for twelve, ninety six pieces
platters plus gravy boat

Mom's gone but her precious china carries
daily servings of scrambled eggs, soup or strawberries
so much wasted energy protecting the goddamned dishes
I'm happy to set them free.

Praise on Father's Day

Praise the beads of sweat along my father's brow as he repaired
my red bike on a hot summer's eve

Praise campfires at Lake Seneca where Dad fried bacon in Mom's
discarded iron skillet Sunday mornings in July

Praise the tree house Dad built in the backyard next to the
chicken coop where I climbed and read my favorite books

Praise puppies Dad placed in my old playpen keeping them safe
from over-anxious cousins

Praise orange pumpkins Dad skillfully carved into jack-o-lan-
terns on All Hallow's Eve

Praise jump ropes Dad patiently turned with Francine's Dad,
talking of Roger Maris' home runs as we skipped Double Dutch
loops

Praise every schoolbook Dad neatly covered each September
with brown paper grocery bags

Praise the Woody Dad taught me to drive, shift and change its oil

Praise stories Dad told of Depression, World War II and
Frank Sinatra at the Paramount

Praise generosity and kindness Dad offered others, stopping to change every flat tire noticed along 95 from Jersey to Florida

Praise the mountaintop Dad showed me with his personal view of the world

Praise Dad's struggle with addiction and anxiety that kept him prisoner all those years

Praise lessons learned about coping and surviving when life gets rough

Praise Dad's tormented spirit and broken heart

Praise Dad's strength, triumphs, gifts along with his troubles, so he may find eternal peace.

Honorable Mention, Connecticut Authors and Publishers Association
Winter 2012

Sisters by Law

Sisters in law
connected by Tom
husband, kid brother
celebrated countless occasions
and meals setting spoons,
forks, knives, Grandma's best dishes
washing, drying
traveling Garden State's
eighty-eight miles north
linking two families
at special Sunday dinners

Sisters by law
drive south to the shore
summer parties
little neck clams
crabs from old buckets
grilling steaks
sip frozen daiquiris
in canvas seats circling the patio
every August dragged playpens
umbrellas and five kids
across hot sand
eating pizza for dinner
on Seaside's boardwalk
bringing home bags
of salt-water taffy

The sisters in law
two women
connected by law
on an aqua painted bench
drinking rum and Pepsi
remembering triumphs
and disappointments
sharing memories, lost hopes
and family secrets
Love never mentioned
but always between them.

Sacred Home

Tear-wet eyes
strain to see
green patchwork
from a small plane window

Ancestry from other lands
pumps through my veins
yet, Irish triumphs
my anointed name
Maggy, descendant of Brian

Arriving Ireland
thirteen February
two thousand two
boots planted firmly
as rare winter snow
dusts my blown kiss
toward my sacred home.

Nature

Magnolias

Breathing morning's dew
magnolias curtsy
before my window frame
treasuring scent-filled blooms
before week's end
since pink petals drop
delightfully
just as they arrive
stitching garden quilts
to enjoy 'til fall.

Barna Woods

Ah! scent of faeries
enchanted woods
magic smell and glistening dew
chartreuse carpets cover rolling hills
like comfy winter quilts
sunshine filters through treetop crowns
ferns bow to the wood mouse
darting cross my path
adored woodland
safe haven, sanctuary

Moss tightly wound around tree trunks
like bandages wrapped on soldiers' wounds
craggy tree roots reach
like old fingers grabbing earth
decomposing leaves turn to muck
soggy path beneath my feet
as molasses mud coats my boots
protection of dark forest
eventually leads me into light

Mystical refuge:
Barna Woods

Emily's Bird

He bit
and ate
he drank dew
he stirred a crumb

Unrolled and rowed home.

Erasure poem based on Emily Dickinson's "A Bird Came Down the Walk".

Clearly Ocean

"How inappropriate to call this planet earth
when it is quite clearly Ocean" ~ Arthur C. Clarke

Roaring
crashing
salty tongue
lashes sandy beaches
horizon hinges ocean depths to the sky
while moon calculates tomorrow's tides
glimmering sunrise
seagulls hover
sandpipers poke
running just in time
not to be knocked
by its surge
transports shells, seaweed
rare message in a bottle
brought to shore
quickly sucked back
again
again
and again.

Winter Moon

A white circle pasted into December sky
illuminates lavender kissed frozen hills
pine tree boughs heavy with snow
create Christmas card scenes along my way

Icicles grip snow-covered roofs
watching full moon glide into stillness
gazing, dreaming...
somewhere south
a warm tropical isle.

Death

Saint Paul's

Death rolled into view
sons and grandson escorted Ann's casket
up the aisle of Saint Paul's
Visiting hospital Ann wasn't
the vibrant gardener, comical woman I loved
suffering a broken wrist, tracheotomy
confused, barely knowing me
My grief began

Ann was Mom's best friend
then mine
sharing shock of her abrupt exit
twelve years since Mom's funeral
the last time I sat here
I was baptised at Saint Paul's,
Sunday School, confirmed
this was grandmother's church
mother's church
my church, till marriage
familiar, comfortable, at home
yet service, creeds and hymns
modernized over years I did not attend
made me feel like a stranger
uninvited, unwelcome.

Fini

Over
fini
last scene
lights out
door shut
curtain closed
the end
no bickering
or laughs
no more bills
diets or
laundry
no worries
no fears
no cough
aches or meds
silent sobs
dried tears
heartache
reluctant farewells
no breathe
no life
death
quiet
now dark
see obit page 8
she died
fini.

My Mother Died

My mother died and my planet crashed
others predicted loss and pain
I would be different, stronger, braver
we weren't buddies, confidantes, barely friends
a superficial relationship in her sober years
weekly obligatory telephone calls
visiting monthly for Sunday pot roast dinners
never depth to our conversations.

My mother died and my world crumbled
she never mentioned loving me
never jotted it in a note or card
no, "I love you"
at the end of a chat
never said how great I looked
when I lost twenty pounds
barely noticing as I gained it all back.

Mother died and my heart is draped in sorrow
I never saw breakfast on the table
or had eyes watching when I climbed the school bus
newly polished shoes were not by my bedroom door
I did that myself
although cream cheese and jelly sandwiches
were prepared the night before
between sips of rum and coke
from her pink polka dotted glass.

My mother died and I felt abandoned
alone, scared, like when I was five
sitting on cold December steps
outside a locked kitchen door
as she entertained her handsome
Marine friend returning from Korea
when Dad was on business in Florida

Regret and pain since my Mother died
no chance now for reconciliation
healing or mending deep family wounds
never expressing the unrevealed love between us
I never expected feelings of grief
my sudden fear of death
almost worse fear of life
my Mother died and life will never be the same.

Life

Star Money

Sky bucks
star money
fire dollars
hip disciples
follow the crowd
fill up on lattes
un-thinkers
globalization groupies
brand worshipers
Jim Jones wannabees
substitute caffeine
for cool aid
under the guise of
a green lady

Order please
can you remember
"java lava chip
mocha brûlée
frappachino
café misto grande
with a splash of
soy milk"

Five bucks, please
pay to be a Star.

Summer of Lemons

Thoughts of lemons
instantly puckers my lips
medicinal, miracle fruit
self-contained package
cleans marble, squeeze on fish
soufflés, zest
sore throat remedy

Cups of sugar, filtered water
sixty four freshly pressed lemons
a standing invitation to local bees
lemonade sales boom
on hot boardwalk days
sticky counters
swatting bees
many, many bees
intermittently flirting with
Seton Hall fraternity boys
under July sun

Mornings at the beach
spritzing lemon juice on my hair
imitating California surfer girls
before chemicals and sophistication
took over innocent teen years
slice open, flick seeds away
suck on one
you'll see
it's tart.

Toast

Obsessed
I am
with toast
it's what I love
to eat the most

Smear with butter, cheese
or jam
make a sandwich
eggs and ham

Don't serve me cold
or warm bread
only hot, crispy, brown
toasted, is what
I want to be fed

Lucky, Lucky Girl

Center of my world: *my room*
not really a room, a dressing room
walk-in closet without a door
Great-Grandma's twin maple headboard from Cherry Street
pushed against the pink plaster wall
at bedtime I dove into a cozy sea
running my fingers around the labyrinth of chenille
exploring as I fell into dreamland

My prized possession: *skate key*
dangles from a string around my neck
like a family heirloom
freedom to travel beyond my block
on eight metal wheels
jumping curbs sailing on sidewalks
to school, back, town, back
no parents, no borders, no boundaries
only me in charge of my eleven year old life

Best part of my world: *the yard*
rose bushes, fig trees, grape vines
rectangles of grass covered with dandelions in spring
red leaves in fall, snowflakes piled high in winter
my playground
'round back doghouse for Spotty and Blackie
climbing tree, secret clubhouse
no cares or worries in my world
lucky, lucky girl growing up in the 1950s.

My Tribe

Four hundred fifty six days ago I left my tribe it wasn't a sudden or rash decision it was planned practical thought out, now I go through my day from spot to place wandering without support or reassurance from people like the ones I knew by the lake of beauty, no one here to say hello communicate lend a hand if I need it as in the childhood place of my daughters, where mothers and fathers gathered sharing children's growth goals dreams sprinkled with disappointments defeats, where I fought for the library to keep the high school band to ban neon signs from ruining our rural hamlet, members of my tribe knew what I thought what I wanted how I operated where I worked who I was and how I lived, respectful and trusting of them as they were of me, the editor handyman butcher dentist postman old timers members of my tribe all standing for something, having passion purpose together on our little piece of the planet, in my daily life now uncertainty and occasional isolation, I look for permanence and seek a new clan to carry me forward.

Art

Van Gogh et Gauguin

Vincent Paul invite à peindre dans son studio le sud[2]

Van Gogh and Gauguin
paint with heart and hand
passion nurtures poetic collaboration
confidantes creating autumn scenes
on cold canvases of mutual respect

Falling leaves, yellow-oranges, violet-blues
squeezed onto palettes of artistic brotherhood
feed each other's imagination
test form, color, technique, brush strokes
laying the foundation for Modern Art

Fraught with angst
Vincent's paintings do not sell as Paul's
drunk, Vincent cuts part of his ear
terrified, Paul abruptly leaves

Yet, the relationship survives
letters of admiration end only
with Vincent's death
leaving his far reaching influence
enormous spirit and body of work

[2]*Vincent invites Paul to paint at his studio in the south*

Oh William!

"Words, words, words." Hamlet, Act II, scene ii

In a blue chair on a blue floor
pen clutched tightly in hand
nothing in my mind
of words, I've lost command

Ideas don't come
my mind a blank void
no idea for a poem
I'm frustrated and annoyed

Interrupting my blank sheet
a familiar, bearded gent
who is this man
how was he sent?

Suddenly I realize
it's my mentor, the bard
I know him oh so well
Shakespeare's walking in my yard

Who follows him
Ladies Montague and Capulet
extending her gloved hand
"I don't think we've ever met"

My high school years
filled with plays and prose
extensive memorizations
I've forgotten how they go

Characters mostly sinister
full of jealousy and deceit
dysfunction in their families
none being too discreet

William penned thirty-seven plays
I'm familiar with a few
learning Hamlet, senior year
"Speak the speech I pray you"

Julius Caesar sophomore year
beware the Ides of March
more memorizations
my throat was very parched

Shylock, Lady Macbeth
most disturbing of the lot
love doesn't conquer all
we learned from Juliet and Romeo's plot

"William, can you help me
get through this writer's block
my poetry group meets tonight
I'm fighting 'gainst the clock"

"No, my Lady, find your own words
create a sonnet, haiku or ditty
your language doesn't resemble mine
tis a crime and dreadful pity"

William is departing
walking across the grass
am I imagining all of this?
Keep writing, get to class!

Breakfast Pandemonium

Pedestrians
   zig
     and
   zag
avoiding eggs frying on sizzling July sidewalks
Tropicana flows into gutters and drains
toast drips with butter and jam clogging crosswalks
coffee splashes from trash cans on street corners

I want breakfast!

Bursts of color from unlikely fireworks
reflect on morning skyscrapers
merchants, ad men, brokers, bike messengers
traveling down Lexington Ave

I'm battling the crowd!

Sidewalks to the brim with chaos
no air, panting, no breath
taxis honk, buses beep, delivery men curse
pollution: air, noise

I'm freaking out!

Busboys, waitrons, short order cooks
armed with trays and spatulas
ignoring pleas, my stomach growling

I'm starving!

Clashing with commuters, I reach the secret
underground passage of Grand Central
all I wanted was a bagel with cream cheese
New York city mornings are pandemonium

I forgot!

*Inspired by the Modern painting "The Liver is the Cock's Comb" (1944) by
Arshile Gorkey*

About the Author

Janice O'Brien

A self-proclaimed chatterbox, Janice O'Brien was born when Sun and Mercury were in Gemini, creating her strong drive for self expression and communication. She is a poet, writer and designer living on the Main Line outside of Philadelphia.

Over her professional career, Janice was an Art Director, Package Designer, Brand Manager and Marketing Director, all requiring extensive business and promotional writing. She is a member of the Main Line Writers Group and Off Line Poets.

*Writing a book of poetry is like dropping
a rose petal down the Grand Canyon
and waiting for an echo. ~ Don Marquis*